Published by Ladybird Books Ltd
A Penguin Company
Penguin Books Ltd, 80 Strand,
London, WC2R 0RL, England
Penguin Books Australia Ltd, Camberwell,
Victoria, Australia
Penguin Group (NZ), cnr Airborne
and Rosedale Roads, Albany,
Auckland 1310, New Zealand
All rights reserved

2 4 6 8 10 9 7 5 3 1

Ladybird and the device of a ladybird
are trademarks of Ladybird Books Ltd

Printed in China

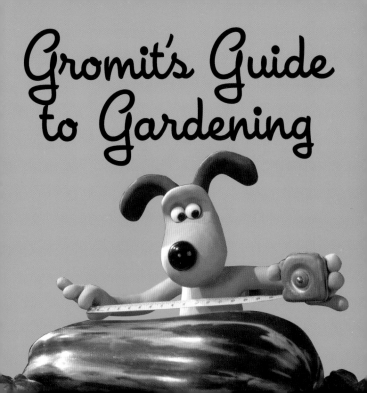

Gromit's Guide to Gardening

Greetings gardeners !

When it comes to growing fruit and vegetables, Gromit's the top dog. Many a day he's found tucked away in his greenhouse, pruning, nurturing and cultivating.

In this book he passes on a bumper crop of tips for gardeners everywhere.

From how to protect your vegetable plot from the ultimate vegetable-destroying machine
- the rabbit -
to hints
on growing
marrows
worthy of the
greatest vegetable
show. So dig in!

Feel the benefits of a vegetable

Gardening is a joyous experience. It gets you out of the house and away from the stresses and strains of everyday living. When it's just you and your vegetables, problems and frustrating owners just fade away.

The first steps towards a glorious garden

Any size garden or greenhouse will do when growing vegetables and fruit, but bigger is definitely better. Ensure it's a nice, sunny spot with good drainage, and with easy access from your home. And keep dirt to a minimum – there's nothing worse than muddy paws all over the house.

'...my secret garden!'
Lady Tottington

Get some protection

Ensure that your vegetable plot has full protection from local wildlife, particularly in the form of the vegetable-munching rabbit. Erect a secure, rabbit-proof fence, preferably with Anti-pesto alarms to alert you to any intruder. If in doubt, it's always best to send in the professionals.

Avoiding accidents

Maintain the highest levels of safety in your garden, particularly if those close to you are a little accident-prone. Always use shatterproof glass in your greenhouse and, in order to prevent slippery accidents, regularly clean paths to remove moss, cheese crumbs or ground-in crackers.

It's tool time

Equip yourself with decent gardening tools. Spades, forks and rakes are vital weapons in the gardener's arsenal - but try not to leave them lying around. And remember to keep them locked up at night, away from prying neighbours.

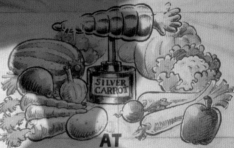

GIANT VEGETABLE COMPETITION

SILVER CARROT

AT
TOTTINGTON HALL

FUN FAIR AND ~~FUN~~

5 days of propagation to go!

Making the most of your garden (with particular reference to marrows)

Watching your very own plants or seedlings grow into luscious fruits or vegetables is a thrilling experience. And once you've mastered the basics, there's nothing like a local vegetable show to allow you to show off your little marvels.

'I dunno, vegetable mad this lot!'
P.C. Mackintosh

Start with the basics

When planting, firmly press in plants or seedlings with your paws. Don't forget to label your plants or make a note of their names and locations.

Weed and water your vegetable patch regularly. In hot weather and in the build-up to an important show, it's important to give your garden a good soak morning and night.

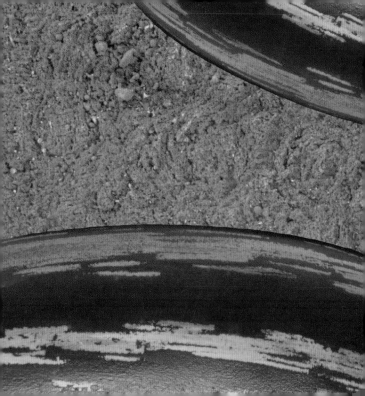

Get into compost

Your fruit and vegetables need nutritious soil if they're to grow big and healthy. Incorporate lots of organic manure and fertiliser. You could even make a compost bin for your garden.

Good stuff to add: old newspapers, cheese rind, uncooked vegetable peelings, Wallace's old woollens, tea bags.

Bad stuff: dog bones or any cooked food scraps, cracker wrappers, polyester or synthetic tank tops, toast, jam.

Sleep well my beauty

Early in the season you can protect new plants from the cold by covering them with a layer of horticultural fleece, a woolly tank top or even an electric blanket*. Or, for individual plants, cut off the bottom of a plastic fizzy drinks bottle and cover.

*Not strictly advisable.

Keep them peeled

It's a good idea to inspect your vegetable plot on a regular basis so you can check for any weeds or vermin problems (or are just in need of a good excuse to get out of the house). Barking at your plants is also beneficial to growth.

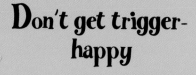

Don't get trigger-happy

There's no need to resort to violence when dealing with rabbits as there are plenty of humane ways to deal with them. A simple sack or a more elaborate trap in the form of the 'Bun-vac' is more than adequate when dealing with the blighters.

'Say your prayers, Big Ears!'
Victor

The Marrow
(CUCURBITA PEPO)

The marrow is a wonderful plant with large, solid fruits that can be used immediately or stored for several weeks (in preparation for that local vegetable show). With its pretty striped skin and hefty fruits, the 'Tiger Cross' variety is a particular favourite as it can be relied upon to impress the socks off any competition judge.

Go deep for goodness

Choose a sunny but sheltered spot for your marrow with well-drained, moist soil. The addition of well-rotted manure or garden compost will give best results. Dig it in as deep as you can, but don't get carried away.

'How's that prize marrow of yours coming on?'

Wallace

Drink up

Once the plants are in flower and when the fruits have started to swell, they will need plenty of water*. In hot weather, they might need as much as two gallons a day.

* Generally, water is preferable to Wallace's left-over tea.

Look after your darlings

Once the marrow starts to crop, the rate
at which they form fruit is phenomenal.
Fully-ripened fruits should
be cut with a long stem
and kept under lock and
key (far away from scheming
neighbours, hungry rabbits
or clumsy owners) at
45-50° Fahrenheit.

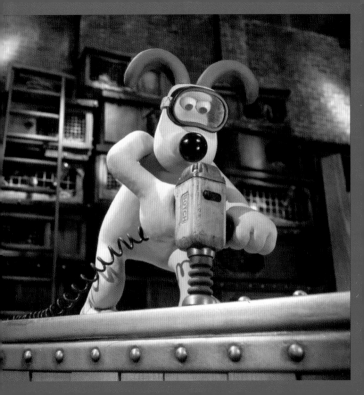

It's all about accessories

A well-placed gnome or decorative urn can add a touch of elegance to any garden. It also helps if your lawn is a mile square.

Gardening tips from over the fence

Gardening attracts a huge cross-section of society and is a wonderful uniting force for different people to meet and discuss their passion for plants.

On the other hand, something as simple as a local vegetable show can sometimes engender extreme competitiveness and deep resentment amongst normally sane and law-abiding people. Try to keep a level head and sense of perspective when partaking in any kind of local contest.

All things bright and beautiful

Many find that a little 'spiritual' help in the form of prayer or even the sprinkling of holy water can result in home-grown miracles (particularly when it comes to bumper crops of carrots).

'Let them grow big and strong under thy loving care...'

Rev. Hedges

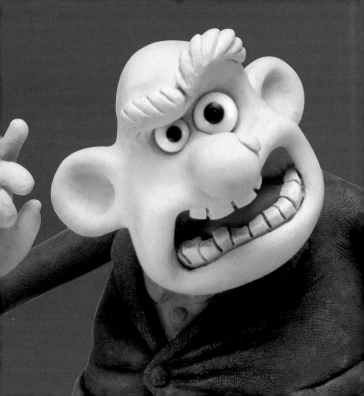

Search and destroy

If you want to rid yourself of slugs (and avoid the likes of the Great Slug Blight in '32 when they were apparently the size of pigs), your best bet is to bury containers of beer in the soil around your plants. They'll be attracted to the smell, fall into the containers, and end their days in a sozzled stupor.

Aim high

Good growing conditions and a bit of tender loving care can lead to produce of quite magnificent proportions, as Lady Tottington's sumptuous 'Carrotte de Chantenay' amply illustrates. Totty's glorious turnips are also the talk of the town.